THE ORPHAN MUSES

D1366339

THE
ORPHAN
MUSES

The Orphan Muses
first published 1995 by
Scirocco Drama, an imprint of J. Gordon Shillingford Publishing Inc.
Reprinted February 1999
©Michel Marc Bouchard, 1988
English Translation ©Linda Gaboriau, 1993
Originally published in French as
Les Muses orphelines, Leméac Editeur ©1989

Cover design by Terry Gallagher/Doowah Design
Author photo by Robert Laliberté
Translator's photo by Guy Borremans
Printed and bound in Canada

We acknowledge the support of The Canada Council for the Arts
and the Manitoba Arts Council for our publishing program.

Canadian Cataloguing in Publication Data

Bouchard, Michel Marc, 1958-
[Muses orphelines. English.]
The orphan muses
A play.
Translation of: Les muses orphelines.
ISBN 1-896239-04-8

I. Title. II. Muses orphelines. English.
PS8533.O7745M8713 1995 C812'.54   C95-910265-5
PQ3919.2.B68M8713 1995

To my sisters Luce, Caroline, Claudine…
in loving memory of Josée…

My Picture Book

Ten years ago, I was writing *Dans les bras de Morphée Tanguay*, a satire about child-rearing. A dark, psychedelic look at the family and the education system. This play proved to be the genesis of *La Contre-nature de Chrysippe Tanguay, écologiste, La Poupée de Pélopia, (Pelopia's Doll)*, and *Les Muses orphelines* (*The Orphan Muses*).

In the Tanguay series, I compare myself to a painter who over the years pursues a study of the same images, the same colours, the same preoccupations. I'm pleased to invite you to the vernissage of the fourth painting in this egotistically personal series. A fourth painting coloured by the past, by desertion and by family secrets. A questioning without censorship, without a real answer, of the fateful core of our existence: our family, our genesis.

Characters

CATHERINE Tanguay: The eldest sister, 35 years old. Elementary school teacher in Saint-Ludger de Milot.

ISABELLE Tanguay: The youngest sister, 27 years old. Employee at the gate to Dangerous Passes Road.

LUC Tanguay: Their only brother, 30 years old. Pseudo-writer.

MARTINE Tanguay: The middle sister, 33 years old. Captain in the Canadian Armed Forces, stationed in Baden-Solingen, Germany.

Set

Saint-Ludger de Milot, in the Lac-Saint-Jean region of Québec. April 1965. The set evokes the sitting room-dining room in a two-story country house. The front door opens into this room. A dining room table. Some chairs. An electric organ.

Production Credits

Les Muses orpelines premiered on September 7, 1988, at the
Théâtre Aujourd'hui, Montreal, with the following cast:

CATHERINE .... Anne Caron
ISABELLE .... Dominique Quesnel
LUC .... Roy Dupuis
MARTINE .... Louise Saint-Pierre

Directed by André Brassard
Assistant Director: Roxanne Henry
Set and Costumes designed by Meredith Caron
Props designed by Louise Campeau
Lighting designed by Paul Mathieson
Musical supervision by Pierre Moreau
Sound Track: Patrice Saint-Pierre

The English translation of *Les Muses orphelines* was commissioned
by the Banff Playwrights Colony and workshopped at the Colony
in June 1993. It was first produced by Ubu Repertory Theater in
New York, in December 1993.

The English-language production in Canada of *The Orphan
Muses*, directed by David Ross, opened at the Western Canada
Theatre Company, in Kamloops, on January 20, 1995, and at the
Belfry Theatre, in Victoria, on April 4, 1995.

Translator's Note: The text presented here includes the revisions
made to the script by the playwright, prior to the second
production at Théâtre d'Aujord'hui in 1994.

Michel Marc Bouchard

Michel Marc Bouchard is one of the leading voices of the new generation of Québécois playwrights. He has written over twenty plays including *La Contre-Nature de Chrysippe Tanguay, écologiste, La Poupée de Pélopia (Pelopia's Doll)*, *Les Grandes Chaleurs (Heat Wave)*, *Les Feluettes ou La Répétition d'un drame romantique (Lilies or The Revival of a Romantic Drama)* and *L'Histoire de L'oie (The Tale of Teeka.)* Bouchard is the recipient of many awards, including the National Arts Centre Award, the Dora Mavor Moore and Chalmers award. His plays have been translated into several languages and extensively produced abroad.

Les Muses orphelines (Grand prix littéraire du Journal de Montéal and Prix du du critiques de théâtre de l'Outaouis) has been published in a European French translation, by Noëll Renuade, by Théâtrales in Paris, and in an Italian translation, by Francesca Moccagatta, by Ubu Libri in Milan.

Linda Gaboriau

Linda Gaboriau has translated more than forty plays, including the works of some of Québec's most prominent playwrights including Michel Marc Bouchard, René-Daniel Dubois, Normand Chaurette and Gratien Gélinas. Her translation of Bouchard's *Les Feluettes* (*Lilies*) was nominated for the Governor General's Award for literary translation and won the Dora Mavor Moore, Chalmers and Jesse Richardson Awards.

ACT ONE

(Holy Saturday. Late afternoon. CATHERINE, puffing on her cigarette, takes inventory of the contents in a woman's suitcase.)

CATHERINE: Three scarves, three red scarves, two blouses with polkadot prints.

ISABELLE: *(Enters from outside, carrying a bag.)* I lost track of the time.

CATHERINE: *(Stubbing out her cigarette, furtively.)* Close the door! Damn sand! We're gonna end up buried alive...

(CATHERINE closes the door.)

ISABELLE: It takes half an hour to walk into the village.

CATHERINE: It's not a broom you need to keep this place clean, it's a shovel.

ISABELLE: I got your ham. *(Beat.)* I lost track of the time. It happens.

CATHERINE: Twenty-seven years old and you don't know how to close a door. You waiting for the whole hillside to move into the house before you close the door? Some inheritance! Honest to God! Ten acres of sand with a house on top of a hill Ma called Calvary. Ten cold, windy acres of sand, and a twenty-seven year old girl who still doesn't know how to close a door.

ISABELLE: I got your ham.

CATHERINE: There must've been some change.

ISABELLE: The ham was four twenty-three. You gave me five bucks. Here's your seventy-seven cents.

(CATHERINE takes the change.)

You're not running off to hide it? You should buy me a gun. Walking back from town with a fortune like that, it's pretty risky.

CATHERINE: You owe me your pay cheque. You're late on your board. One…three…six pairs of socks: the red ones, the blue ones…

ISABELLE: *(Opening the door.)* Nobody came while I was out?

CATHERINE: Use your head! A car out here is the event of the year.

ISABELLE: Get off my back, Catherine. I lost track of the time!

CATHERINE: Don't tell me you went out like that, in the middle of spring thaw! *(Beat.)* "An ounce of prevention is worth a pound of cure."

ISABELLE: "Best cure, stay pure." "Practice prevention, avoid detention." God, I bet the kids at school make fun of you.

CATHERINE: If Ma could hear you.

ISABELLE: She can hear me, don't worry. She can hear me.

CATHERINE: Close the door! *(ISABELLE closes the door, but continues to look outside.)* Two fans…. I've counted everything three times now, and I'm still missing a Spanish skirt.

ISABELLE: He's wearing it.

CATHERINE: Don't tell me he went into the village dressed like that again! I didn't see him leave.

ISABELLE: How come you're going through Ma's clothes?

CATHERINE: Did you see him in the village?

ISABELLE: I hate it when you answer me with another question! No, I saw him down at the foot of the hill. He was writing. How come you wanted me back before supper?

CATHERINE: You have to go back to the village.

ISABELLE: What am I, your workhorse? Take your car!

CATHERINE: I have to cook the ham.

ISABELLE: I'm expecting company.

CATHERINE: Who?

ISABELLE: Company!

CATHERINE: You're going to take this suitcase to the thrift shop. I couldn't give it to you before, with him hanging around.

ISABELLE: Oh, sure! We'll do it behind his back, and he'll hate my guts when you tell him I'm the one who got rid of Ma's clothes!

CATHERINE: Just take the suitcase. Before he comes back. If he knows it was you, he won't make a scene. I don't know how many times I've warned him that I'd get rid of these rags if he left the house in them. He can dress up all he wants...here at home.

ISABELLE: We haven't seen hide nor hair of him for three years...

CATHERINE: He'll take off again, and he'll forget all about this place...

ISABELLE: You could make an effort and get off his back.

CATHERINE: ...but what about us? We're stuck living here with these people who have memories like history books.

ISABELLE: He says we inspire him. He says we're his "muses." Muses are women who help people find ideas. That's what he says. And he says we're going to help him finish his book, "Letters from a Spanish Queen to her Son."

CATHERINE: When? He's been working on it for ten years now! Longer.... He was eleven years old when I told him he'd do better to write what was going on in his head, instead of dressing up like Ma. God, I shouldn't have been so understanding. A good slap in the face, that's what, then dump the suitcase at the thrift shop! Get going, before he comes back. Go on!

ISABELLE: Burn it. Throw it out!

CATHERINE: What if Ma heard you?

ISABELLE: She can hear me.

CATHERINE: Ma never missed a chance to play the organ, every Sunday, every holy day, year in and year out. We can't burn her clothes during Lent! *(Silence.)* Why did you ask him to come back? If you're hoping to get some money out of him, forget it. He doesn't have a cent.

ISABELLE: God, you're a pain about money. I missed him.

CATHERINE: I'd rather miss him than have to deal with him here. I spent years telling the whole village that he'd changed.

ISABELLE: What a liar!

CATHERINE: I even told them his book was about to come out. I'd finally convinced them he might not be as crazy as they thought. And then you had to get him to come back. Things weren't extravagant enough for you.

ISABELLE: Wait a minute. *(She exits.)*

CATHERINE: Isabelle, get going before it's dark out. He'll be back any minute now.

ISABELLE: *(She returns with a pencil and a little notebook.)* "Extravagant?" What does that mean?

CATHERINE: Put something on, you'll freeze!

ISABELLE: What does "extravagant" mean? "When you know what words mean and how to use them, you're freer, and you're closer to the truth." That's what he says.

CATHERINE: "Extravagant" means something excessive, unreasonable, fantastic. Like extravagant spending. Extravagant behaviour.

ISABELLE: Well, that's true. When he's around, things stop being reasonable. "Extravagant", with an "x"?

CATHERINE: That's right, an "x."

ISABELLE: E. X. T.?

CATHERINE: E. X. T. He doesn't belong here! B. E. L. O. N. G.

ISABELLE: I'm warning you, if you tell him to leave, I'm leaving with him.

CATHERINE: Look at the way he behaves, you know as well as I do, he's not the right company for a young lady.

ISABELLE: Suddenly I'm a young lady. Guess it's better than being a ree-tard.

CATHERINE: He's sick, Isabelle.

ISABELLE: The mood you're in, guess it's been a while since you showed your bum to your boyfriend, eh!

CATHERINE: Isabelle! You shouldn't talk to your sister like that on Holy Saturday!

ISABELLE: Who you going out with now? Oh yeah, Dr. Lemieux. I guess he spends his life looking at bums. You dropped Sergeant Claveau for a doctor. You're moving up in life. You've gone through just about every profession in Saint-Ludger! What a family! A sicky, a mongoloid and a slut!

CATHERINE: Isabelle, come over here! Sit down. *(Dangerously gentle.)* What's the matter, Isabelle? You're usually so considerate, so sweet...

ISABELLE: So dumb, so retarded...

CATHERINE: Isabelle.... Catherine's going to tell you something, but I don't want to have to repeat it.... Isabelle...

ISABELLE: Here we go, the big words, the tears in your eyes.... If you can't do your own dirty work, don't ask other people to do it for you. I'm not gonna get rid of the suitcase, you hear me?

CATHERINE: A little respect! Today's Holy Saturday, Isabelle.

ISABELLE: God, you're a pain. So it's Lent. Big deal. Tomorrow we'll have indigestion from too much ham and too much chocolate. Does that make it such a special day of the year, I should suddenly show you some respect?

CATHERINE: Do I have to remind you of everything I've done for you since Ma's death? Ungrateful brat!

ISABELLE: Ungrateful! Ungrateful! I knew we'd get to that word sooner or later. Don't bother telling me what it means. I have a whole page full of what that damn word means.

CATHERINE: I didn't mean it.

ISABELLE: I wasn't close enough for a slap in the face!

CATHERINE: It just came out, before I could stop it.

ISABELLE: Lots of things have come out of you, before you could stop them. Whenever something makes you mad, you hit me with your famous last words, using Ma's remains. You've used Ma's dead body once too often, Catherine. Tomorrow's Easter. A good day for resurrections.

CATHERINE: What's that supposed to mean?

ISABELLE: So nobody came while I was out?

CATHERINE: So you refuse to go to the thrift shop?

ISABELLE: Stop answering me with more questions!

CATHERINE: No, Isabelle, nobody came while you were out. Use your head. You refuse to go? (*CATHERINE picks up the suitcase.*)

ISABELLE: Stay here. We can play poker. We're expecting company.

CATHERINE: I've got better things to do than entertain your ghosts, Isabelle.

ISABELLE: Go ahead, don't get sidetracked. Go take the sicky's clothes to the poor so they can look crazy too.

LUC: *(Voice off.)* Thanks a lot! *(Enters dressed in the missing Spanish skirt.)* They're real gentlemen, those policemen.

CATHERINE: Policemen!

LUC: They come around and open the car door for you, they help you out...

CATHERINE: Now what have you done? Close the door!

LUC: *(To CATHERINE.)* You leaving on a trip, Catherine? Put that suitcase down.

CATHERINE: You know what people around here call a guy who dresses up in his mother's old rags.... Never mind, we'll try to forget their word for it.

LUC: I told you to put that suitcase down. You can take it back to my room. If you try to get rid of it again, I'm warning you, what I just did in the village will seem tame compared to what I'll do next time.

CATHERINE: *(To ISABELLE.)* You said you saw him at the foot of the hill! Liar!

LUC: I went to visit Madame Tessier at the post office.

CATHERINE: I don't believe you. She was closed today!

LUC: I went in through her kitchen. The minute she saw me, she tensed up, got stiff as a board. "Madame Tessier, my mother forgot something here a long time ago. Do you remember? I was with her. I was ten years old."

ISABELLE: What did she say?

LUC: She said that Ma came on a Maundy Thursday when the post office was open, but today's Holy Saturday and the post office is closed.

CATHERINE: She's right, you had no business going there today.

LUC: Then it was my turn to tense up, and I told her she just might have to make an exception today.

CATHERINE: Don't tell me you threatened her?

LUC: I told her I'd never gotten rough with a woman before, but I just might have to make an exception myself. She turned white as an envelope and she followed me into the backroom of the post office.

CATHERINE: You did threaten her!

LUC: I leaned on the counter, graciously—

ISABELLE: Graciously?

LUC: 'Graciously' means the way Mama knew how to behave, 'with elegance,' not like the lady lumberjacks from around here. "Madame Tessier, twenty years ago my mother came to pick up a package she'd received from Québec City."

ISABELLE: What was in the package?

LUC: A Spanish dictionary.

CATHERINE: Isabelle doesn't need to know all that!

LUC: When Ma asked for her package, Madame Tessier had already opened it.

ISABELLE: How come?

LUC: There was a war going on and we had a foreigner living in our house. She figured that gave her the right to open our mail. She told Ma she read too much, that too much reading was bad for you, and that Spanish looked like a real pretty language, even though the only word she knew was *corrida*, but she didn't know what it meant. So Ma decided to explain to her what the word *corrida* meant.

ISABELLE: Ma explained that to Madame Tessier?

LUC: Yeah, and since she's the kind who gets lost in a blueberry patch, Ma practically had to draw her a picture.

CATHERINE: Show some respect for you elders.

ISABELLE: Go cook your ham, Catherine!

LUC: Mama explained that a *corrida* was like having

some farmer invite everyone in Saint-Ludger to the hockey rink to watch him kill his bull. She explained that in the middle of the rink there was the toreador—the toreador was like the local farmer dressed up in fancy upholstery material. Ma's patience was put to a test. She had to explain everything, step by step. How the toreador waved a big red curtain called a *muleta* and that drove the bull crazy. How the bull would charge the *muleta*, and keep missing it, and everyone from Saint-Ludger would shout "Olé!" When the bull had charged and missed dozens of times and was getting out of breath, and people were fed up with shouting "Olé," the toreador would stab the animal with big knitting needles!

ISABELLE: Madame Tessier must've laughed?

CATHERINE: Not at all.

LUC: She got all choked up with her ugly thoughts and spit them out in Mama's face, saying that it took a loose woman who slept with foreigners to shout "Olé" when a farmer killed his bull.

ISABELLE: She said that to Ma?

CATHERINE: Filthy rumours!

LUC: Mama came home in tears. I was running behind her, saying "Your package, Ma! You forgot your package."

ISABELLE: And how did things end today?

LUC: After refreshing her memory about the little *corrida* scene, I told Madame Tessier that I refused to leave her post office empty-handed. It was the Spanish dictionary or her chignon.

CATHERINE: More threats?

LUC: So twenty years later, she took a little book covered with dust out from under her counter. (*LUC takes the little Spanish dictionary out from under his skirt and hands it to ISABELLE.*) "Don't be late for the Easter vigil tonight, Madame Tessier, I wouldn't want you to miss the sequel."

ISABELLE: So how did she react?

LUC: She was pretty shaken, but she had enough strength left to call Sergeant Claveau. He's the one who "escorted" me home.

ISABELLE: *(Thumbing through the Spanish dictionary.)* It sounds so beautiful when you talk, Luc.

CATHERINE: What do you intend to do at Easter Vigil?

LUC: I just told you. The sequel.

CATHERINE: You're still not satisfied? Madame Tessier today, your tantrum at the grocery store yesterday, crying your eyes out because they didn't have the makings of a paella. It's useless reminding them of all that, Luc. Nobody cares about it any more. It was twenty years ago. Forget it!

LUC: Forget it. Forget that bunch of filthy minds who dragged our mother through the mud?

CATHERINE: When Ma...died, they decided to let bygones be bygones. You should do the same with them. Forget it.

LUC: I don't want to forget! I can't forget! I need to bug those pious souls who love to remind you that when you were a poor orphan, they used to bring you a box of groceries at Christmas and a bag of rags every spring...and you were their ticket to a good conscience. I want to remind them of their responsibility in our little family drama. They're here, stuck in my brain like a clot, blocking my imagination.

CATHERINE: Write about what you'd like to do to them. It's not so dangerous.

LUC: My writing is too precious for me to waste it on a bunch of illiterates. Writing means going beyond...until I've settled Mama's unfinished business with them, I'll never be able to pay her the homage I owe her.

CATHERINE: There are so many other beautiful subjects that could inspire you.

LUC: I don't feel like rewriting Maria Chapdelaine's romance in the wild, just to make you happy. Jesus Christ!

CATHERINE: Swearing during Lent is a sacrilege!

ISABELLE: God, you're a pain with your neat little sentences. Jesus Christ! Stop interrupting him! That's what I missed. It's so beautiful when he loses his temper. *(Looking at the Spanish dictionary.)* It's always so *extravagante.*

CATHERINE: You should take a rest, Luc. Your nerves are shot. *(She takes back the suitcase and heads towards the door.)* You'll end up with a nervous breakdown.

ISABELLE: Where you going with the suitcase?

CATHERINE: Do you remember how to cook the ham?

ISABELLE: I hate it when you answer me with another question!

CATHERINE: I've always saved us, Isabelle.

LUC: The suitcase!

CATHERINE: *(Leaving the suitcase.)* I'm going to apologize to Madame Tessier, poor old lady!

LUC: Sure, go apologize for being my sister.

> *(CATHERINE exits. We hear the car start up. LUC takes out a manuscript and starts writing.)*

ISABELLE: Did your tantrum "inspire" you? *(Beat.)* When are you gonna let me read your book?

LUC: Soon.

ISABELLE: Right now, okay?

LUC: Not right now. Soon.

ISABELLE: You want to see the notebook with all my words? And correct my mistakes? *(She hands him her notebook.)*

LUC: *(Reading.)* You still writing by ear? "Extravagant" has an "a" not a "u." "Deliverance"—to take groceries to people's homes?

ISABELLE: Lionel Fraser's the one who said that when I bought the ham. He said: "You want me to deliver that to your house? We got free deliverance."

LUC: It's "delivery" for groceries, Isabelle, not "deliverance." Gotta be more selective about who you ask what words mean. *(She yanks her notebook away from him.)*

ISABELLE: You think I'm a mongoloid too, don't you?

LUC: Don't say that! *(Gently.)* "Deliverance" is a word. It means helping someone out of an unpleasant place or situation.

ISABELLE: Monday we can leave for Montreal together.

LUC: Give me back your notebook. I haven't finished correcting your words.

ISABELLE: Monday you're gonna take me with you.

LUC: Give me your notebook!

ISABELLE: If you say yes to Monday.

LUC: Monday's two days away. Lots of things can happen between then and now.

ISABELLE: When you send me those long love letters from Montreal, they're imaginary letters, right? Don't bother, you're wasting your paper on me.

LUC: Don't say that!

ISABELLE: I wrote to you because I missed you and I wanted you to come back. But you came back just to make the whole village sweat it out...not to see me, not to "deliver" me!

LUC: Don't say that, Belle. Luc loves you, big love, like the dam on the Peribonka! That's pretty big, eh?

ISABELLE: Leave me alone! I'm not seven years old any more. You're gonna take me with you, right? Just for a week?

LUC: (*Playing his mother.*) Tonight Mama's going to the Easter Vigil. She's going to climb the stairs to the organ loft. She's going to push fat Madame Claveau off the bench and play…. (*He sits down at the electric organ and plays and sings.*)

                "Una canción me recuerda a aquel ayer"

ISABELLE: You're gonna take me to Montreal with you!

LUC: "Cuando se marchó en silencio un atardecer,
                Se fue con su canto triste a otro lugar,
                Dejó como campañera mi soledad,
                Una paloma blanca me canta al alma…"

ISABELLE: (*At the window.*) It's Monsieur Savard's taxi. Luc, go hide.

LUC: How come?

ISABELLE: We'll surprise Martine!

LUC: (*Stops playing.*) Martine?

ISABELLE: I called her in Germany yesterday and asked her to come home.

LUC: How come?

ISABELLE: Go hide, you'll find out later.

                (*LUC hides. ISABELLE sits down at the organ and sings, to the tune of "La Paloma."*)

                "If at your window you see a gentle dove
                Treat it with care, and welcome it there with love
                It may be I, so do not deny its plea
                Crown it with flowers, grant love its hours for me."

                (*MARTINE enters dressed in civilian clothes and carrying her suitcases. She's exhausted.*)

MARTINE: Sounds like Ma singing.

ISABELLE: Leave the door open.

MARTINE: *(Shaking ISABELLE's hand.)* Isabelle!

ISABELLE: Martine!

MARTINE: Too bad we have to see each other again on such a sad occasion. *(She takes ISABELLE into her arms.)*

ISABELLE: It's all right, Martine. You can let go of me. Catherine doesn't want you to hold me too much. She says it's not normal for two women to smooch together.

MARTINE: In the taxi, Monsieur Savard didn't even know.

ISABELLE: You told Monsieur Savard?

MARTINE: Yes.

ISABELLE: You weren't supposed to. He didn't want anyone to know. He wrote it...in his will.

MARTINE: How did he die?

ISABELLE: Dr. Lemieux doesn't know yet. Dr. Lemieux's Catherine's new boyfriend.

MARTINE: Sickness? An accident?... Suicide?

ISABELLE: Catherine doesn't want us to say words like that in this house.

MARTINE: How come Dr. Lemieux was taking care of him? I thought he was in Montreal? Was he visiting here?

ISABELLE: Yeah.

MARTINE: I got on the plane in Stuttgart yesterday afternoon. I couldn't sleep. You know what time it is in Germany right now?

ISABELLE: I can't even keep track of the time here.

MARTINE: Where's he being laid out, at the sacristy or the school?

ISABELLE: He didn't want to be laid out.

MARTINE: Where's Catherine?

ISABELLE: If you'd arrived on time, you would've seen her. You said five o'clock!

MARTINE: I'm a half hour late on a twenty-hour trip! Besides, the bus from Alma to Saint-Ludger isn't the most reliable, and taxis are pretty rare around here.

ISABELLE: Still, it's a drag for the people who are organizing things!

MARTINE: How come Catherine didn't come to meet me at the bus?

ISABELLE: She's taking care of the funeral arrangements for tomorrow.

MARTINE: I'm going to take a bath.

ISABELLE: Martine, did you love Luc?

MARTINE: I know you had a lot of admiration for him. Personally, I always found him a bit strange.

ISABELLE: You could wait till he's six feet under before you shit on him.

MARTINE: Look, you must be old enough to understand that I didn't have to love him, just because he was my brother.

ISABELLE: I'm too dumb to understand things like that.

MARTINE: Let's just say I never considered him essential to my happiness.

ISABELLE: "Essential." What does that mean?

MARTINE: Something necessary, something important…

ISABELLE: "Essential." (*Writing the word in her notebook.*) This is my notebook for words. I feel like I don't have enough words. I try to use every new word once a day. (*Beat.*) So how's the war going over there?

MARTINE: *(Faint smile.)* There's no war where I am.

ISABELLE: They usually send soldiers where there's a war.

MARTINE: Baden-Solingen is a strategic base…

ISABELLE: What does "strategic" mean?

MARTINE: Isabelle, I don't have the strength to explain every word I use.

ISABELLE: You could make an effort. I haven't seen you for four years.

MARTINE: I'm tired. *(Beat.)* How have you been? Must be lots of guys hanging around you these days?

ISABELLE: Only when I go square dancing. I got other things to take care of before I start thinking about guys.

MARTINE: I don't really like being here. It feels macabre.

ISABELLE: "Macabre?"

MARTINE: It means "pertaining to death," "something sad or grim." Aren't you going to write it in your book?

ISABELLE: It's not a pretty word. I only like joyful words, words that are "grandiose," "splendid," "en-rap-turing."

CATHERINE: *(As she enters.)* The door's wide open! Who cares? Catherine'll pay for the heat! Madame Tessier refused to come to the door. I passed Monsieur Savard's taxi on my way back…. *(She turns around and finds herself facing MARTINE. Unenthusiastically.)* Martine? What a nice surprise! *(MARTINE goes to hug her.)* Sorry, I've never been much for hugs and kisses.

MARTINE: That's a shame.

CATHERINE: So you decided to spend Easter with us. You could've warned me.

MARTINE: You getting cynical in your old age? If you're not capable of showing some emotion at tragic moments like this, you're colder than I thought.

CATHERINE: What's so tragic?

MARTINE: Death doesn't affect you any more?

CATHERINE: Don't tell me you've become more Catholic than the Pope! He died at three o'clock yesterday and he'll rise from the dead tomorrow, like every Easter Sunday.

MARTINE: Who are you talking about?

(LUC enters.)

LUC: So you crossed the Atlantic to come cry over my grave?

MARTINE: Is this some joke?

LUC: That's you all right—the dead meat specialist.

MARTINE: A joke!

(Beat.)

You got me to cross the Atlantic for a joke?

CATHERINE: Can someone tell me what's going on?

MARTINE: Isabelle called me in Germany yesterday so I could come to Luc's funeral.

CATHERINE: No!

ISABELLE: I missed her!

MARTINE: I spent the last twenty-four hours in a black hole and now I find out it's a joke. Twenty-four hours of remorse about everything we've been through together.... "Remorse," write it down, Isabelle. It's not a pretty word but it's apt to be useful in any language. It means, deep and painful regret, it means feeling goddamn guilty...

ISABELLE: "Remorse," with an "c" or an "s."

MARTINE: Somebody buy her a dictionary, for chrissakes!

LUC: How's the war going? When are you going to come

back to Saint-Ludger with a Russian's head strapped on the top of your tank like antlers?

MARTINE: I swore I'd never come back here!

CATHERINE: Nobody's normal in this family. We have to live with it.

ISABELLE: Catherine says I have a behaviour problem.

LUC: You should've worn your soldier's uniform, we could've played Ma and Pa.

MARTINE: I'm never going to play that game again, Luc! (*Beat.*) Aren't you ever going to grow up, the lot of you? (*Silence.*)

CATHERINE: It's been a long time since the four of us were together. Could I offer anyone a drink?

MARTINE: Why not! Drag out the photo albums. Let's try laughing at how we looked back then. Family get-togethers stopped being my idea of a good time years ago! When you leave home, you start looking ahead and family becomes a thing of the past. The only intense moments we'll share now are when we're closing the lid on someone's coffin. I just missed one of those memorable moments today.

LUC: Aren't you glad to know I'm still alive?

MARTINE: I closed your coffin on the plane on the way over here, and it was a relief.

CATHERINE: That's an awful way to talk.

MARTINE: I thought I could stop worrying about Catherine who's spent her life putting up with your moods, your crises and your financial problems.

CATHERINE: Mind your own business, Martine.

MARTINE: She sold the land, the barn…the cottage to finance the inspiration of the male in the family. She mortgaged herself to the hilt so that Monsieur could experience Europe. So he could make his dream come true. He wanted to write! Write a book nobody's ever read a line of.

LUC: A real little soldier! You like to see your enemies dead.

ISABELLE: (*Sincere and delighted.*) I never knew anyone who could insult people as good as Martine!

MARTINE: Isabelle, if Catherine never taught you any manners, I will. There are other ways of letting your sister know that you love her and you miss her.

LUC: You got money problems, Catherine?

CATHERINE: Martine's the one who said that.

LUC: But it's true!

CATHERINE: It's personal. And my personal affairs are nobody else's business. Isabelle, come over here. You better find some way to make Martine forgive you.

ISABELLE: How come?

CATHERINE: (*As she slaps her.*) Ungrateful brat!

ISABELLE: Ungrateful! You've all hidden behind Ma's corpse too much. You've used it so much there's nothing left for the worms. So much she's decided to rise from her grave and come back to straighten things out around here. Tomorrow's Easter, resurrection day.

     (*ISABELLE exits.*)

CATHERINE: The door, Isabelle. Poor child!

MARTINE: You want to pity her or hit her? Make up your mind!

CATHERINE: I only do it because I love her.

MARTINE: Good thing you don't hate her!

LUC: She's never known how to handle her.

MARTINE: She can't exactly call you a success either.

LUC: Watch it, you goddamn butch soldier, if you don't shut up—

CATHERINE: Luc, why don't you take your Spanish skirt off first!

LUC: Federico gave it to Mama.

CATHERINE: Stop talking about Ma!

LUC: He sent her a whole suitcase full of them.

CATHERINE: *(To MARTINE.)* Ever since he came back.... I'm not responsible for my actions.

LUC: She looked so beautiful in this skirt.

CATHERINE: Ever since he's been back, I can't control Isabelle. Sometimes, I feel like hitting her, hitting her so hard we'd forget everything...everything we did to her.

            (To LUC.) Yes, it's true. I'm up to my ears in debt because of you. This year I'm teaching first grade and second grade just to make ends meet. And if I have any spare time, I substitute teach in grade five. Don't think I gave you that money so you could write.... I gave it to you so you'd stay away from Isabelle. So you'd stop putting ideas into her head. I'd teach gym if I thought I could get rid of you once and for all. And don't get any ideas, you're not gonna take her with you to Montreal. *(Beat.)*

            She's acting so strange these days. You heard what she said: Ma's gonna rise from her grave, that she's gonna come back, she's gonna rise from the dead on Easter Sunday. So when I don't know what else to invent to defend us, I hit her.

MARTINE: Stop feeling guilty about it. It's all right what we told her. We were just kids...

CATHERINE: Remember how pitiful she was, huddled in the corner of her room in the dark? And she kept repeating: "When's she gonna come back? When? Her trip to Spain is taking too long. Too long."

MARTINE: She hadn't eaten for two days. The three of us were ready to burst into tears. And she kept repeating....

"When's she gonna come back? When?" Then the letter arrived.

LUC: "Dear Children, I asked a travelling companion who was on her way home to mail this letter from Québec City so it would reach you sooner. I will not be coming back. I have gone to join Federico. Don't look for me..."

MARTINE: "Don't try to find me..."

CATHERINE: "Perhaps some day you'll understand. Adios..."

LUC: "Adios!"

MARTINE: "Adios!" *(Beat.)* It's touching to see us like this. The only time we show any emotion is when we act out that goddamn story. Like vultures feeding off carrion!

CATHERINE: It is touching. *(Silence.)* How are things in Germany?

MARTINE: Great! *(Silence.)* Have you finished your book yet?

LUC: Almost! *(To MARTINE, who's laughing.)* What's so funny?

MARTINE: Sorry! I can't stop picturing you in your grave.

(They all laugh.)

CATHERINE: I'm going out with Dr. Lemieux these days.

MARTINE: You want to know who I'm going out with? *(Silence.)*

LUC: I was happy to see you, Martine. I had to meet you head-on, I had to attack, but I was happy...

CATHERINE: I'm happy to see you too. *(She opens her arms.)*

MARTINE: *(Doesn't respond.)* So, how do you like being rejected?

CATHERINE: Emotions don't last long with you!

MARTINE: I thought you would've told her. It was your responsibility, as her guardian.

LUC: She didn't want her to know. It was easier for her to play mother, if the kid didn't think that her real mother might come back to get her some day.

CATHERINE: If you're going to shit on people, there's a mop in the kitchen.

MARTINE: I was hoping she was no longer the kid everyone pitied, the village retard. I even figured she would've met some guy.

CATHERINE: As if a guy could solve a woman's problems. It takes a lesbian to say something like that.

MARTINE: You must have swallowed too much sand. You talk like a dried-up old maid.

LUC: Looks like we're going to need the mop. Welcome to Saint-Ludger! Charming little hamlet of seven hundred souls, more commonly known as "the ass end of the   dead end."

CATHERINE: How can you tell the truth to a twenty-seven year old woman who acts like an eleven year old who has tantrums no one can control? Am I supposed to apologize for spending the last twenty years of my life making her believe her mother died in Spain? Was I supposed to admit that she's still alive and that she simply abandoned us? "Don't try to find me. Never try to find me. Perhaps some day you'll understand." Well, the day I understand how a mother can abandon her children, I'll explain it to her.

MARTINE: Guess I didn't come back for nothing. You need a soldier to send to the front lines? Here I am. I've been trained to clean up other people's shit without asking any questions. Twenty years ago, I inherited the job of telling her the big lie we'd invented.... It'll be my pleasure to tell her the truth today. Then never ask me to come back here again. I'm gonna make sure I forget all about you, even your names.... *(She calls.)* Isabelle!

CATHERINE: What you don't know can't hurt you.

(ISABELLE enters soaking wet, and holding a bouquet of thistles.)

The door, Isabelle!

(CATHERINE goes to close the door. ISABELLE walks over to MARTINE and hands her the thistles.)

MARTINE: Thank you, Isabelle. I forgive you.

ISABELLE: I never said I was sorry. Put the "burrs" in water, they're not for you.

MARTINE: *(Preparing her speech.)* Isabelle…

ISABELLE: What does "strategic" mean?

MARTINE: It means something that's part of a strategy, a plan.

ISABELLE: Like you. *(Beat.)* So you find it hard to take, Martine, someone who's supposed to be dead but isn't? A long time ago, you were the one who came into my room to tell me Ma had died in Spain. The three of you were standing there with these tragic looks on your face…. Well, a month ago a lady phoned here. A lady who spoke really well, with lots of beautiful words. I didn't understand them all. She wanted to know how we were.

I told her that Catherine was a school teacher and that she was going out with a doctor, that Martine was a captain in the army in Germany, that Luc was going to publish a book…and that I was nothing, just the dumb girl who works at the gate where they count the logging trucks that enter Dangerous Passes Road.

LUC: Mama phoned here?

ISABELLE: And I realized I was nothing because I never got to hope that some day I could report to a lady like that. I never thought the dead could return to earth.

MARTINE: Is she making this up again?

CATHERINE :   No, I can tell when she's making things up.

ISABELLE: How do you think you react when you find yourself talking on the phone with your mother who died twenty years ago and you can't even understand all the words? Eh? I bet no dictionary in the world has a word for how you feel! She was disappointed in me. You hear me? She was disappointed because I didn't have anything to tell her. Because I hadn't "emancipated," that's what she said. "Emancipated." And Catherine told me "to emancipate" meant to "grow up." She asked me to get you all together here. The "burrs" are for Ma. She'll be here tomorrow...and I haven't had time to learn enough beautiful words.

MARTINE: Ma's gonna be here tomorrow?

CATHERINE: Did she tell you why she was coming back?

ISABELLE: No. And I'm still trying to understand why she left. Guess I better catch up.

MARTINE: Ma's gonna be here tomorrow?

LUC: She'll be here tomorrow!

                 (*The phone rings four times. CATHERINE goes to answer it.*)

CATHERINE: (*Into the phone.*) Hello. Yes, just a minute. It's Madame Talbot. She wants to know when Luc's funeral is. Who wants to answer?

LUC: (*Taking the phone.*) Madame Talbot? It's Jacqueline Tanguay here! I'll be arriving tomorrow!

                 (*End of ACT ONE.*)

ACT TWO

(Holy Saturday. Evening. ISABELLE enters from outside, carrying funeral wreaths. She arranges a few in the living room and exits to take one to a bedroom. She comes back. CATHERINE enters. She's carrying a package. She notices the wreaths.)

ISABELLE: They're for Luc. They didn't know where to make the "delivery." They left them on the porch. They're still afraid to come into the house. Guess they didn't know where to send them. It's "macabre," eh? That one's from the ladies at the library. That one's from the Saint-Ludger Recreation Committee.... We put one of them in your room, the one from your buddies at school. Luc says we should make them into bouquets for Ma. Leave the door open!.... Please. *(CATHERINE leaves the door open.)*

CATHERINE: I hate the sound of the wind whining in the cypress trees.

ISABELLE: When the snow started to melt and the weather got warmer, Federico always asked us to leave the door open. He'd sit on the porch and sing his songs with his guitar. He used to say that back home, in his country, the doors are always open. That way the air can circulate and chase away bad thoughts. That's one thing I remember about him.

CATHERINE: *(Closing the door.)* What I remember is how he used to make us freeze. Where is everybody?

ISABELLE: In their rooms. Martine said she was having trouble with her "jet log." They must be thinking about what they're gonna say to Ma.

(CATHERINE lights up a cigarette.)

ISABELLE: When did you start smoking?

CATHERINE: Ages ago. I didn't want to set a bad example for you.

ISABELLE: Can I have one! *(CATHERINE offers her a cigarette.)* At the gate, the guys all smoke Export A's. *(ISABELLE lights up.)* I like menthols. Have you thought about what you're gonna say to her?

CATHERINE: Poor Madame Tessier had palpitations after listening to Luc's little scene about the *corrida*.

ISABELLE: So did you go show your bum to the doctor?

CATHERINE: *(Surprisingly candid.)* Yes. I needed a bit of consolation.

ISABELLE: "Consolation." Oh, forget it. I'm tired of asking what words mean. I got so many to learn, one more or less won't make no difference, she'll still see that I'm just a dummy.

CATHERINE: Don't say that, sweetie.

ISABELLE: "Sweetie?" I'd like to know what that word means when you use it.

CATHERINE: It means what it means. A sign of affection. You want me to bring you a beer?

ISABELLE: Two signs of affection in the same sentence, something's fishy. You're not supposed to drink during Lent.

CATHERINE: Well, sometimes you can negotiate with God! Isabelle, I'm going to tell you something, but don't make me repeat it.

ISABELLE: Here we go. One of your emotional sentences.

CATHERINE: I just want to tell you that I love you, Isabelle. You're my little girl.

                There, I said it. Here's an Easter present for you.

                (ISABELLE opens it.)

ISABELLE: A dictionary!

CATHERINE: I stopped by the school. I've got the keys. I stole it…. It's even got illustrations.

ISABELLE: There are so many words, where do I start?

CATHERINE: "Reconciliation," maybe you can start with the word "reconciliation."

ISABELLE: You've never been any good at poker. You always show your hand too soon. It's gonna take longer than one night for me to forgive you.

CATHERINE: I love you!

ISABELLE: You had years to prove it. But instead, you called me every name in the book, you never let me do what I wanted, you never gave me a cent and once I had some money, you started charging me board. You never helped your "little girl" act like a woman, and when she tried, you made fun of her. Do I have to remind you of what you did a couple of months ago? The night you sent your old boyfriend, Sergeant Claveau, after me?

CATHERINE: A trucker. You didn't realize how dangerous it was.

ISABELLE: A trucker or a doctor, what's so dangerous if he makes you feel good…. I had fun with my trucker—and maybe your policeman got there too late.

CATHERINE: It's my duty to protect you.

ISABELLE: Tomorrow you're gonna have to explain yourself to Ma.

CATHERINE: What's this address in Montreal that Dr. Lemieux wants to give you?

ISABELLE: He had no business talking to you about that!

CATHERINE: What's this all about? *(Beat.)* Isabelle, I love you!

ISABELLE: I think you got worse vocabulary problems than me.

(LUC enters, dressed in another Spanish skirt and a few accessories.)

LUC: Give me the car keys.

CATHERINE: Where do you think you're going decked out like
                that?

LUC: To church.

CATHERINE: Over my dead body. I'm not letting you out of here
                dressed like that.

                (She rushes over to block the door.)

LUC: The car keys!

CATHERINE: Never!

ISABELLE: *(Referring to the Spanish dress.)* You chose the
                prettiest one!

CATHERINE: I don't mind here in the house. But not at Easter
                Vigil!

LUC: Isabelle, where does Catherine hide the car keys?

CATHERINE: Ma will be here tomorrow!

LUC: Precisely. I want everyone to have paid for what
                they did to her by tomorrow.

CATHERINE: You've taken enough revenge already!

LUC: Where are the keys, Isabelle?!

CATHERINE: Isabelle, I swear, there's gonna be hell to pay, if you
                tell him where the keys are!

LUC: All right, I'll walk.

CATHERINE: *(Calling.)* Martine! Martine, come help me!

ISABELLE: Luc, what are you gonna say to Ma tomorrow?

                (MARTINE enters dressed in her uniform.)

CATHERINE: Martine, he wants to go into the village dressed like
                that!

MARTINE: I'm not the family bouncer.

CATHERINE: Stop him!

MARTINE: Let him go, I don't give a damn.

ISABELLE: What are you gonna say to her, Luc?

CATHERINE: They'll kill you!

ISABELLE: Luc, what are you gonna say to her tomorrow?

CATHERINE: *(As she hands him the keys.)* All right, go ahead! Get yourself killed!

ISABELLE: Answer me, Luc!

CATHERINE: Go ahead!

ISABELLE: Luc!

CATHERINE: We've already got the flowers for your grave.

ISABELLE: What are you gonna say to Ma, Luc?

LUC: *(To ISABELLE.)* Will you give me a break with your retarded questions!

MARTINE: Luc!

    (Silence.)

LUC: *(Realizing he has hurt ISABELLE. Beat.)* Sorry! Look at me, Belle. I didn't mean to say that.

ISABELLE: But you said it. You said what everybody thinks. Retarded.

LUC: I feel ridiculous. *(He takes off a few Spanish accessories, including the mantilla.)* If you love me, look at me. *(She looks at him.)* I'm sorry.

    Do you forgive me?

    (Beat.)

ISABELLE: What are you gonna say to Ma tomorrow?

LUC: I'm going to give her my book.

ISABELLE: Really?

CATHERINE: Have you finished it?

LUC: Yes.

ISABELLE: Can you read us some of it tonight?

LUC: I have to go to church.

CATHERINE: Just read a bit of it. Here…in the house. We'd really like that, wouldn't we, Martine?

MARTINE: Sure.

LUC: *(Heading for the door.)* I've got the Easter Vigil.

ISABELLE: It goes on for four hours. You can go later.

MARTINE: You mean that book actually exists?

(LUC opens the door. We hear the wind.)

The wind! His book's gone with the wind!

(LUC closes the door and goes to get his book.)

LUC: Stay right there!

CATHERINE: *(Whispers.)* Thanks, sweetie!

ISABELLE: How come?

CATHERINE: Now he's going to stay home.

ISABELLE: *(Loudly.)* I didn't get insulted just to make you happy.

(CATHERINE starts arranging the chairs.)

MARTINE: Luc's book, Ma coming back! I guess I didn't come this far for nothing.

(The three sisters are obviously excited.)

CATHERINE: Everybody have a seat!

ISABELLE: Martine, you sit here.

CATHERINE: Anyone want popcorn?

ISABELLE: Me!

MARTINE: Go easy on the butter.

ISABELLE: Don't listen to her.

MARTINE: And don't let it burn!

              (LUC re-enters.)

LUC: *(Calmly.)* Forget the popcorn!

MARTINE: Is there any beer?

CATHERINE: Cold or room temperature?

MARTINE: Room temperature.

ISABELLE: Cold.

LUC: Could everybody just settle down! This isn't the Saturday night movies. This is my life's work.

MARTINE: Oh, excuse us!

ISABELLE: That's beautiful, what he just said. *(She sits down with her dictionary and her notebook on her lap.)*

CATHERINE: *(Whispering.)* Go ahead, Luc. We're listening.

LUC: "Letters from a Queen of Spain to her Beloved Son."

ISABELLE: Your title's longer than it was yesterday.

LUC: *(Reading.)* "Dear Reader, This book contains all the letters which betray my mother's silence. The silence where she buried her unfulfilled desires, her aborted dreams. I had the mission of putting this silence into words. Her life was my inspiration. I have dissected her memory, spied on her destiny. I have transformed her, I have worshipped her and magnified her. I have turned her life into my liberating work of art." Prologue.

ISABELLE: What's a "prologue?"

CATHERINE: Write it down and look it up afterwards.

ISABELLE: I need to learn them in "context."

CATHERINE: *(Exasperated.)* Isabelle! *(Beat.)* Go ahead, Luc, we're listening.

LUC: (*Reading.*) "First letter from Canada. 20 January 1944. Dear Son. Tonight, on the hillside, the wind has crystallized waves of snow, like a sea where the ebb of the tide suddenly stood still. Two dark knights on horseback emerge from this sea beyond time. I recognize my husband, my duty. And there's the other one, beside him, mystery and the unknown. As he turns his gaze on me, this stranger says: "*Buenas tardes, Señorita.*" He could have said "I love you" and I wouldn't have felt more embarrassed. I lowered my eyes. It was as if he'd mysteriously made the statue of the toreador a cousin once brought back from a trip come to life. That plaster matador with his perfect body made me doubt my devotion to Christ, so thin and emaciated. I fear I am a woman who prefers the *muleta* to the cross. Federico Rosas will board in our house during the construction of the dam on the Peribonka River. Lots of love, Mama."

"11 May 1944. Dear Son, Spring is back...and so is the sand. Federico has been part of the family for more than three months now. Isabelle loves to play with him. Yet she still cries whenever he smiles at her. Catherine is becoming more and more flirtatious with Federico and Martine more distant with me. And you ask too many embarrassing questions at the supper table."

MARTINE: Ma, how come you only go fishing with Federico? How come you close the doors to the sitting room at night? How come Pa's been sleeping in the attic?

LUC: (*Reading.*) "He's learning to speak French better all the time. I bought him a little notebook so he could keep a record of his new words."

ISABELLE: Like me.

LUC: "Yesterday I played the organ at all three masses. The priest gave the same sermon all three times. He says that to learn a foreigner's language is to sell our soul to the devil."

MARTINE: Move ahead in time! We know all that!

ISABELLE: It sounds nicer when it's written.

LUC: "Yesterday Catherine went for a walk with Federico. Since that walk, she's stopped being flirtatious with him, and she's stopped speaking to me."

ISABELLE: What did you talk about on your walk, you and Federico?

CATHERINE: *(Defensively.)* It's been so long. I don't remember.

ISABELLE: Did you talk to him about your bum?

CATHERINE: May I remind you that you haven't had your quota of slaps today.

LUC: "At night, the smell of his skin, the taste of his lips.... I'm struggling with my desire, with his desire."

CATHERINE: We can do without those details, Luc.

ISABELLE: Have a beer, Catherine.

LUC: *(Reading.)* "Madame Claveau has been replacing me more and more often at church. The priest saves the weddings and baptisms for me. He rattles on about the innocence of children and our duties as parents. Catherine has been taking care of Isabelle more often, as if she was trying to keep her away from me. Martine has joined the Cadets. She's away every weekend. And you are spying on me. Studying my every move. Your loving mother."

"3 July 1944. Dear Son. Last night we went to the organ party."

ISABELLE: The organ party!

CATHERINE: The church wardens had organized a party in the Knights of Columbus hall to finance a new organ...

LUC: *(Reading.)* "They want me to play something. I don't have anything to wear!"

ISABELLE: You could wear one of the dresses Federico gave you!

LUC: (*Playing his mother.*) I'll wear the white one. The white one with the mantilla.

MARTINE: She had absolutely no sense of decency!

LUC: (*Playing his mother.*) Your father can't come to hear me play. He says he can't take the time off.

ISABELLE: But Federico's coming, isn't he?

LUC: (*Playing his mother.*) Of course, sweetie!

MARTINE: No decency.

CATHERINE: When we arrived at the Knights of Columbus Hall, the party had already started. We could hear everyone singing along with Florence Giroux. She was doing La Bolduc's songs.

LUC: (*Playing his mother.*) Federico pushed open the front doors of the hall and proudly offered me his arm. We walked in together.

CATHERINE: Everyone stopped singing. Even Madame Giroux stopped and since she wasn't used to the mike, everyone in the hall heard her gasp: "She's outta her mind."

LUC: (*Playing his mother.*) The whole village stood there, watching us walk in together. Nothing's as silent as two hundred people being silent. The women lowered their eyes at the sight of the matador. The men lowered their eyes at the sight of the señorita.

ISABELLE: I was holding Luc's hand.

CATHERINE: Martine and I completed the procession.

MARTINE: The head warden tried to relax the atmosphere. He pushed old lady Giroux away from the mike and said: "Welcome to Madame Tanguay and her little brood."

CATHERINE: He missed a great opportunity to keep his mouth shut. We heard a few people laugh.

LUC: (*Playing his mother.*) "Her little brood," just to remind me that I didn't have fourteen kids like all the other women. Four kids wasn't enough to keep a woman busy…. It left her with too much time to get into trouble.

CATHERINE: The head warden tried again. "Welcome to our talented organ player, Mrs Lucien Tanguay."

MARTINE: And he started to clap like a seal.

CATHERINE: Nobody joined in.

LUC: *(Playing his mother.)* Suddenly I felt very peaceful.

MARTINE: The lull before the storm.

LUC: *(Playing his mother.)* Federico helped me up onto the stage. I looked at him as if I was looking at him for the first time. To encourage me, Federico began to hum. After a moment of giddiness, I began to play…

ALL: *(Singing.)*
"Una canción me recuerda a aquel ayer
Cuando se marchó en silencio un atardecer
Se fue con su canto triste a otro lugar
Dejó como campañera mi soledad.
Una paloma blanca me canta al alma
Viejas melancólicas cosas del alma
Llegando del silencio de la mañana
Y cuando salgo a verla vuela a su casa
Donde va que mi voz
Ya no quiere escucharla
Donde va que mi vida se apaga
Si junta a mi no está
Si quisiera volver
Yo la íria a esperar
Cada día cada madrugada
Para quererla mas."

CATHERINE: Two men grabbed Federico. Two minutes later there were ten of them on top of him. People were throwing anything they could get their hands on at Ma: ashtrays, glasses, candles…

MARTINE: And in the middle of all that, there were two kids dancing like Federico had taught them.

CATHERINE: Pa arrived in the middle of the riot. Ma stopped playing.

MARTINE: There was another long silence.

LUC: *(Playing his mother.)* Your father walked to the middle of the hall. Everyone back off and stood against the walls. There was your father, dressed in a soldier's uniform, as dignified as a toreador, standing over Federico, lying on the floor in a pool of blood, like a bull in the middle of the arena, waiting for the final blow. *(To MARTINE.)* Lucien, what are you doing dressed up like a soldier?

MARTINE: No, Luc. Never!

ISABELLE: Play, Martine! Just this once. For the last time. Just for tonight!

MARTINE: No.

LUC: *(Playing his mother.)* Why are you dressed up like a solider?

MARTINE: *(Stands up.)* I'm leaving.

LUC: *(Playing his mother.)* You think that's the solution?

MARTINE: I'd rather leave than go on pretending that it doesn't bother me.

LUC: *(Playing his mother.)* That's so cowardly of you! *(Beat.)* Children! We're going home now!

MARTINE: *(Playing her father.)* No. Stay here. We're gonna settle this right now. You want to show the whole village how happy you are? Well, let's show them the rest.

LUC: *(Playing his mother.)* You knew very well that bringing Federico home...

MARTINE: *(Playing her father.)* I never was able to invent the world you wanted, Jacqueline. I can't teach you anything about my country, it's the same as yours, and you don't even like it. Every morning, we open our eyes and we seem the same trees, the same hillside, the same faces. Maybe I can't talk about love to you.... I learned to say it, but I don't know how to babble about it.... Maybe I'm not...a great...

LUC: (*Playing his mother.*) The word is "lover!"

MARTINE: (*Playing her father.*) Maybe I'm nothing but...

LUC: (*Playing his mother.*) You're just an ordinary guy from Saint-Ludger, like dozens of others. You're just the guy I couldn't choose, because there was no choice. You're just what my children are turning into: ordinary people living ordinary lives.

MARTINE: (*Playing her father.*) Any other guy, another one of your dozens of guys like me, would have killed you by now. I prefer to go kill where it'll count.

CATHERINE: Then he turned on his heels and walked towards the main door of the hall. And just before disappearing forever, he turned and looked at Ma one last time.

MARTINE: (*Playing her father.*) My family warned me. They told me to watch out for beautiful women. It's the devil who gave them their beauty. At birth, he gave them a poisoned present called desire. Jacqueline, you'll always feel desire and it will be your downfall. You better pick up what remains of the Spaniard, his mistress is probably already desiring somebody else.

(*MARTINE turns away from the others.*)

CATHERINE: Thank you, Martine.

ISABELLE: You were really good, Martine.

MARTINE: She better not show up tomorrow saying she's repented!

ISABELLE: What does "repented" mean?

MARTINE: It means someone who comes back on all fours, licking the floor, looking for forgiveness! She's not going to put us through the epitome of pardon! "Epitome" means the cherry on the sundae! Use your dictionary, for chrissakes!

LUC: *(Returning to his book.)* "21 September 1944. My Beloved Son. The autumn winds are sweeping over the hill and there's no escaping the sand. Federico has recovered from his wounds. I received an official letter from the Canadian Armed Forces. Your father is dead. He died in the Normandy landing. His soldier friends had nicknamed him "the suicide case." When I announced the news, Martine smashed the matador statue.

The next day, when she got back from training, Martine aimed your father's old .22 at Federico and froze, as if paralyzed. For her Christmas present, she wants Federico to leave...otherwise, next time, she'll pull the trigger."

CATHERINE: I always wondered, would you have shot him?

MARTINE: No.... I would've shot her. Just wait, tomorrow when we see her walk in the door, we're going to feel vulnerable, like scared little kids, 'cause time's stood still for us since she left. If I see one of you make the slightest friendly gesture, I'll get out the old .22 and this time, believe me, I'll pull the trigger.

LUC: *(Goes on reading.)* "Last letter from Canada. April 1945. Five months have gone by since Federico left. The day he left...*Adiós, adiós!*.... The wind has once again crystallized the snow into immobile waves. This morning I went to the post office to pick up the Spanish dictionary Federico sent me. Madame Tessier was as mean as usual, like the grocer, the priest, the two old maids at the library.... You and Isabelle help me pack my suitcase. I've decided to leave you my Spanish dresses. There'll be other prettier ones where I'm going. Before leaving Saint-Ludger, I'll go sing my liberation at the Easter Vigil. I'll leave the house without kissing you goodbye.... The slightest sign of emotion could undermine my decision. My destiny is elsewhere. Signed: Your mother, who will always love you. Goodbye."

ISABELLE: Goodbye.

LUC: *(Suddenly pushing his manuscript aside.)* They must've reached the blessing of the candles at church. *(He stands up and heads for the door. CATHERINE grabs his manuscript.)*

CATHERINE: What's in the rest of the pages?

LUC: Her life in Spain.

MARTINE: Do you mean you actually believe that she wrote to you after she left? You've been imagining that for the last twenty years?

LUC: Haven't you ever tried to imagine what's become of her?

MARTINE: I tried to forget her.

LUC: How about you, Catherine?

CATHERINE: I didn't have any time to waste on that!

LUC: Are you telling me that you never thought about what your own mother might be doing for the past twenty years? How do you manage to look in the mirror without seeing her in your own features?

ISABELLE: I never had a chance to imagine her. Catherine told me she was in purgatory and since she couldn't explain what purgatory was, well, I couldn't imagine it. The priest tried to explain. He said it was like a long line at the confessional. So I saw her standing in line, waiting, and sometimes I brought her a chair so she could rest.

LUC: I imagined her so clearly that when I finally found her in Spain, five years ago, she was exactly like she was in my dreams.

MARTINE: Found who?

LUC: Mama.

MARTINE: You found Ma in Spain?

ISABELLE: You found her and you never told me?

MARTINE: Is this literature or truth?

CATHERINE: Literature. *(She exits.)*

LUC: When I arrived in Barcelona, I had no trouble finding them. I met Federico on horseback in the middle of their fields. They had a huge estate. Mama was the queen of a huge estate.

CATHERINE: *(Returns with a box full of letters.)* Since Ma's gonna be here tomorrow, there's no sense in trying to hide it from you any more. *(She passes out letters to MARTINE and ISABELLE.)*

LUC: Federico told me Mama was playing the organ at the Iglesia de la Sagrada Familia. I went back into town. When I arrived at the entrance of the Iglesia, I heard the organ.

MARTINE: *(Reading a letter.)* "Hello Catou, I'd like you to send me your father's death certificate..."

LUC: It was so majestic.

MARTINE: *(Reading a letter.)* "I might need it in view of a possible marriage. Love, Mama."

LUC: I hadn't seen her for fifteen years.

ISABELLE: *(Reading a letter.)* "Dear Catou, I'm sending a hundred dollars to buy the children some clothes in view of the upcoming winter. Love, Jacqueline Rosas."

LUC: I walked down the centre aisle of the huge empty church so I could see her in the organ loft...

ISABELLE: *(Reading.)* "Catou, I am enclosing two hundred dollars to help you with Isabelle's education. Ma."

LUC: My heart was beating so fast.

CATHERINE: Read the address in the corner of the envelope.

MARTINE: 102 Saint-Marc Avenue, Québec City.

LUC: She stopped playing.

CATHERINE: She never went to Spain. She made all that up so we wouldn't try to find her.

ISABELLE: My stomach aches!

CATHERINE: Yes, Luc. I thought about her often. Every day. I imagined her sweating in Québec City, in those factories in Lower Town. Having to struggle all day with a sewing machine, making corsets for the ladies in Upper Town…to pay for her desire.

MARTINE: She's in Québec City! Now I can stop wracking my brains. I felt like half my brain had turned into a map of the world, I spent so much time looking for a possible address for her. She's in Québec City.

LUC: Isabelle, go pack your suitcase. We're going to Montreal tomorrow.

CATHERINE: Luc, I've got a thousand dollars in the co-op…. Leave her alone…

LUC: Leave her alone? You sent me half way round the world, you let me believe that Mama was in Spain, just so I'd leave her alone. "Leave her alone!" We left her with you and look what you've done to her! A twenty-seven year old woman with the maturity of a child of twelve and the vocabulary of a telephone book!

ISABELLE: Mind your own business, Luc!

CATHERINE: Tomorrow I don't want to hear any comments about how I've raised her. I gave her everything I could. And she's not going to take her away from me.

LUC: (*Playing his mother.*) I've come back for her, Catou, because I can't stand leaving her here, just waiting for you to have a kid of your own…. Because you know very well you'll never have one. You've gone through every stud in the village but your problem, your little tragedy, is that you're not just sterile in your head. Isabelle, go pack your suitcase.

              (*ISABELLE goes to get her suitcase.*)

CATHERINE: (*Crying.*) I would like to have had twelve kids! Twelve just to get to her, dammit! Twelve just to show her how beautiful a family can be, a real family.

MARTINE: Can you imagine if you had twelve kids? Twelve devastating departures. Imagine asking yourself twelve times why you bothered to sacrifice your life to them…. Turning into a cloying bloodsucker twelve times, so they won't leave…. Twelve thousand sleepless nights because they're gone…. Worrying about their love problems, money problems, career problems. Wondering twelve times over whether you were a good mother, wondering twelve times about the woman you were before they arrived…. Realizing twelve times over that you are nothing but a lousy link in the masterpiece called humanity. Glorious humanity that takes such pleasure in suffering and killing…. I thought our mother was courageous because she dared take off before we did. Imagine…. She didn't even have to feel guilty about me being a lesbian. You can explain that word to Isabelle, Catherine. You can go throw up first, and then explain it to her. I think she's a coward to come back. I don't understand how she can be so masochistic. Or why she needs to know that we really suffered, to know that when we're not hurting each other, we go on hurting inside…

ISABELLE: *(She re-enters with her suitcase and picks up her dictionary.)* "Masochistic?"

MARTINE: Don't bother to look it up. Just look at your brother. The worst kind of "masochist." A real nutcase who's been trying to imitate our mother since the day she left. He's put on the same damn show, every time we've seen him…for the last twenty years. *(To LUC.)* Stop imagining that you're her! Your heroine: "the Queen of Spain." A beautiful book built on thin air! Tomorrow, when you see her and she tells you about the Chateau Frontenac Hotel…and her corset factory, there'll be nothing left to say, nothing to write, nothing to play, because she won't tell the exotic tale you've been waiting for.

ISABELLE: Let's go, Luc!

LUC: No!

ISABELLE: How come? Five minutes ago you wanted to leave.

LUC: No. That's how come.

CATHERINE: Thank you, Luc.

ISABELLE: How come?

LUC: 'Cause you're just a dummy. And I don't see myself stuck in Montreal with a mongoloid.

ISABELLE: Luc, you must know the worst word in the world you can say to someone? Well, I'm shouting it at you right now!

> (*LUC runs out of the house, grabbing the car keys. We hear the car start up.*)

CATHERINE: What's the taxi number? Isabelle, get me Monsieur Savard's number!

MARTINE: He must be at Easter Vigil too.

CATHERINE: Monsieur Tessier told Dr. Lemieux that if he ever saw Luc again he'd have his twins beat him to a pulp.

MARTINE: I don't see what you can do about it. (*Beat.*) Can you believe what we just said to each other and we were stone sober! Any beer left?

CATHERINE: (*After dialling a number.*) Dr. Lemieux must be at church.

MARTINE: I guess God's never been on your side!

CATHERINE: (*Throwing on her coat.*) Go ahead, joke about it. What am I gonna look like walking down the road at one in the morning?

MARTINE: If he kills himself, or if they kill him, or if he dies, don't forget that's what I came home for. It will look better on my leave papers than a resurrection.

> (*CATHERINE exits. ISABELLE comes back with a beer. She hands it to MARTINE.*)

ISABELLE: You want to play poker?

MARTINE: Goddamn crazy family!

ISABELLE: You never would've come if I told you Ma was coming back!

MARTINE: I never wanted to come back here. There's no soul left. I've made a life for myself somewhere else.

ISABELLE: Is it true you never tried to imagine her?

MARTINE: Sometimes. *(Beat.)* I went to Spain too. I didn't look for her, but I felt that she was there.

ISABELLE: Are you afraid to see her again? "Martine made Federico leave. Martine told Isabelle that Ma was dead."

MARTINE: I wish she'd been here tonight to see the damage. You think that's awful? You must think I'm heartless? Isabelle, I've stopped asking myself questions. I've learned to stop wondering why I'm a soldier like my father, why I'm a lesbian, why I get pleasure out of life.

ISABELLE: Martine, do you think that people should have kids?

MARTINE: How can you ask me that?

ISABELLE: Whenever I ask Catherine something, she uses it against me, and Luc has so much imagination, you never know what he'll do with what you say to him. Do you think that it's possible to have a kid and to really love it? Do you think it's possible for a kid to love its mother too? Do you think we're gonna do to our kids what was done to us?

            Do you think people should have kids?

            Do you think it's better to take it out on them, or on the people who hurt us?

MARTINE: *(Touched by the question.)* Not on them.... Not on them....

ISABELLE: I'm gonna cook the ham.

MARTINE: Isabelle, I do feel love for you. You know that?

ISABELLE: I guess that's the only word I know by heart, but I sure would like to have it explained to me again. Most of the time, it seems to mean, I want something.

MARTINE: Not me. I don't want anything from you. Good night.

               (She exits.)

ISABELLE: *(Putting on makeup.)* Ma always used to wear red lipstick...real   red...scarlet.   She   was always...radiant. Ma's clothes were...splendid. Tomorrow,   Ma's   gonna   think   I'm splendid...radiant. I guess everything's ready for Ma's return.

               (End of ACT TWO.)

ACT THREE

(The following morning. Around eight o'clock. Easter Sunday. MARTINE and ISABELLE are busy decorating the table tastefully. MARTINE is in uniform.)

ISABELLE: Stems aren't very long on funeral flowers, eh? I'll tear out some more.

MARTINE: That's enough. We don't want her to think we're congratulating her!

ISABELLE: *(Removing some of the flowers already arranged.)* You're right. Don't want to overdo it. We've already made enough of a fuss.

MARTINE: Pretty, eh?

(ISABELLE places a pitcher of water in the middle of the table.)

ISABELLE: I went to get some spring water when the sun came up. It's Easter water. They say this water stays pure all year. Never goes bad. In a family that's gone bad like ours, a little glass of this water can't hurt. *(Silence.)* Luc and Catherine better show up on time!

MARTINE: Stop worrying.

ISABELLE: They were out all night and they didn't even call.

MARTINE: Don't worry. Nobody called to ask where they were going to be laid out so don't panic.

ISABELLE: I feel real nervous. I've already cried twice since I got up this morning.

MARTINE: You must have good mascara, it doesn't show. You look pretty made up like that.

ISABELLE: I want to show her I've "emancipated." (*Suddenly.*) The ham!

MARTINE: It's all right! You've checked it three times in the last ten minutes. It's gonna start screaming if you stab it any more.

ISABELLE: Where should we have Ma sit? Catherine always took her place.

MARTINE: We can have her sit in the guest's place.

ISABELLE: Ma always spoke so beautifully, eh?

MARTINE: Ma spoke the way people speak in books. Books were her only friends. She'd probably already met Federico in a book before he even arrived in Saint-Ludger. She should've started reading before she met Pa.

ISABELLE: You don't seem so mad at her any more.

MARTINE: Last night I read all the letters she sent Catherine. Cold, practical letters, as if she'd broken all ties with everything here. I still don't understand why she's coming back.... I don't understand.

ISABELLE: Every word I learn opens another door for me...the pretty ones and the not so pretty ones.

The not so pretty ones open more doors than the pretty ones. You just have to get used to hearing them too. I know why she's coming back. She's coming to open the doors that are still waiting to be opened.

MARTINE: You're getting pretty poetic.

ISABELLE: Me? Poetic already? I have to make sure I speak well when she's here. I have to speak as well as her.

MARTINE: You can speak any way you want.

ISABELLE: No. As well as her. (*Silence.*) Do they think women look pretty in that suit?

MARTINE: I'm not a model, I'm a soldier.

ISABELLE: It must be a "strategy" to scare the enemy, eh? You sleep with women?

MARTINE: Yes. With one in particular.

ISABELLE: Two and a half months ago, I met a guy at the gate. He made me feel good.... I guess you must feel as good with her as I feel with him?

MARTINE: I hope so, for your sake. *(They both laugh.)*

ISABELLE: I really like telling dirty stories. It makes me feel better. I guess that's what they mean by "grown-up talk," eh?

MARTINE: Depends upon the grown-ups.

ISABELLE: You're not supposed to talk about that with Catherine. I'd like to talk about it for hours.... It'd be a change from all the stories about our past.

MARTINE: What do you want to start with?

ISABELLE: *(Looking out the window.)* Catherine and Luc are here.

MARTINE: Guess today's not the day we get to talk about sex in this house.

ISABELLE: Luc looks like he's in rough shape.

MARTINE: Thank God! He finally got the beating he deserved!

                   (LUC enters dressed in men's clothes. His head is bandaged, his arm in a sling. He has trouble walking, CATHERINE is helping him.)

CATHERINE: Stop staring like you're watching some sideshow. Come help me.

                   (They help LUC sit down.)

MARTINE: So how was Easter Vigil? Did you bring us a candle?

CATHERINE: Looks like the two of you stayed up all night telling jokes.

MARTINE: *(Sarcastic.)* Looks like the Queen of Spain got one helluva beating!

LUC: *(Barely audible.)* Bitch!

CATHERINE: Shut up, Luc, you'll tear your stitches.

MARTINE: It's been a long time since we've seen you wearing pants.

CATHERINE: Dr. Lemieux lent him some clothes.

MARTINE: He makes a pretty little boy!

LUC: *(Barely audible.)* Isabelle, I want to apologize for yesterday.

ISABELLE: *(Almost shouting as if LUC were deaf.)* What did you say?

LUC: I want to apologize for what I said yesterday.

ISABELLE: I can't understand a thing you say, you're talking like a mongoloid.

CATHERINE: I got there too late. He was sitting in a pool of blood on the church steps. Tessier's twins jumped on him the minute they saw him walk into the church. Luc didn't even have time to go up to organ loft. In no time at all, there were four or five of them on top of him. Then they threw him out on the steps. Barbarians…

LUC: Tell them what you did!

CATHERINE: I had to go into the church to get Dr. Lemieux. When I found him, I realized I was right in the middle of the centre aisle. I don't know why but I stared at them all and began humming. *(She hums "La Paloma.")* The harder Dr. Lemieux tugged on my coat to get me to leave, the louder I sang. I walked out of the church singing at the top of my lungs, and the organist started to play along with me.

MARTINE: You actually did that?

CATHERINE: I felt so good. I felt so good and so free. I had nothing left to hide. I was taking revenge. (*She picks up the suitcase.*) Now there's something else I've wanted to do for ages. (*She walks out the door, only to come back in.*) There's a strange car headed this way. (*MARTINE goes to the door.*)

MARTINE: Anyone else on the road waiting for their mother? The car went right by.

> (*Long wait. ISABELLE is scribbling in her notebook. The clock strikes nine, ten, eleven o'clock, noon. Throughout this time, ISABELLE can be seen getting ready. At noon, ISABELLE exits, then re-enters dressed in a 1940s style suit, she enters with the ham, playing her mother.*)

ISABELLE: Happy Easter, children!

> (*She puts the ham on the table.*)

(*Playing her mother.*) I've been waiting for this moment for so long. I've been dreaming of it for months. Hello, Martine! Hello, Luc! Hello, Catou! The house hasn't changed much.... You worked hard to keep everything the same.

CATHERINE: What is this supposed to mean, Isabelle?

ISABELLE: (*Playing her mother.*) Yes, tell me about Isabelle. (*Silence.*) She isn't here with you? She's in a faraway country? Her work made it impossible for her to come? What has become of her, Catherine? What has she become?

CATHERINE: Not much of anything.

ISABELLE: (*Playing her mother.*) I'd like to thank you for everything you did for her.

CATHERINE: Fuck off!

LUC: (*Making an effort to be understood.*) Does this mean Mama isn't coming?

ISABELLE: (*Playing her mother.*) Here I am, dear.

LUC: The phone call...the phone call....

ISABELLE: The phone call? It was Isabelle's turn to make up a lie.

CATHERINE: *(Sarcastically.)* So, "Ma," where are you arriving from?

ISABELLE: *(Playing her mother.)* I was supposed to come back from Spain but at the very last minute I decided to come back from Québec City. *(She starts to pour water into the glasses.)* Let's drink some Easter water. I won't give you any, Luc, you'll spill it. It's Easter water to purify us. To your health!

MARTINE: I'd love to chat a bit longer, but I've got to catch a plane in Bagotville this afternoon. I'm afraid I don't have time to play. So would you mind telling us why?

> *(ISABELLE sits down on the chair reserved for her mother.)*

ISABELLE: *(Playing her mother.)* Two and a half months ago, Isabelle met a man who told her that the whole village knew that her mother wasn't dead, that she had simply abandoned them. That man was the truth for Isabelle, and today Isabelle is expecting the child of truth.

MARTINE: You're pregnant?

ISABELLE: *(Playing her mother.)* Yes, Isabelle's two and a half months pregnant.

CATHERINE: You wanted to go to Montreal to get rid of the baby, is that it?

ISABELLE: *(Playing her mother.)* Isabelle's baby is a muse. It was the baby who inspired her to do all this. Isabelle preferred to take revenge on you, not on her muse...not on her muse.

CATHERINE: You can't have the baby! I'm going to take you to Montreal!

ISABELLE: *(Playing her mother.)* She's going to have twelve kids, just to show you that children are beautiful.

Twelve who will leave home…. The most beautiful thing about a family is knowing how to leave it!

CATHERINE: You can't do this to me!

(We hear a trailer truck pull up outside and honk.)

ISABELLE: *(Playing her mother.)* You told her how courageous I had to be to abandon you…. Isabelle is abandoning you today.

CATHERINE: Isabelle, I'll sell the house, I've got a thousand dollars in the co-op, we could…

ISABELLE: You can buy whatever you want, Catherine. Don't forget to eat the ham. It's a family tradition.

(ISABELLE exits.)

MARTINE: That's how I imagined our mother…free.

(She exits with her suitcase.)

LUC: I really wish…she had come…for real…. I wanted her to take me in her arms and tell me…

CATHERINE: *(Taking LUC in her arms.)* Don't worry, Luc, Catherine will take care of you. *(Singing softly.)*

"If at your window, you see a gentle dove
Treat it with care and welcome it there with love
It may be I, so do not deny its plea
Crown it with flowers, grant love its hours for me."

The End